HORNET

VS.

WASP

BY
JERRY PALLOTTA
ILLUSTRATED BY
ROB BOLSTER

Scholastic Inc.

The publisher would like to thank the following for their
kind permission to use their photographs in this book:

Page 11: Florin Tirlea/iStockphoto; page 16: Alastair MacEwen/Getty Images; page 18: Biophoto Associates/Photo Researchers, Inc.; page 23: Kent and Donna Dannen/Photo Researchers, Inc.; page 24: top: Staff Sgt. Andy M. Kin/Department of Defense; bottom: Courtesy of Sacramento Hornets; page 25: top: Mass Comm SPC 2nd Class Zachary L. Borden/U.S. Navy; bottom left: Courtesy of London Wasps; bottom right: Getty Images

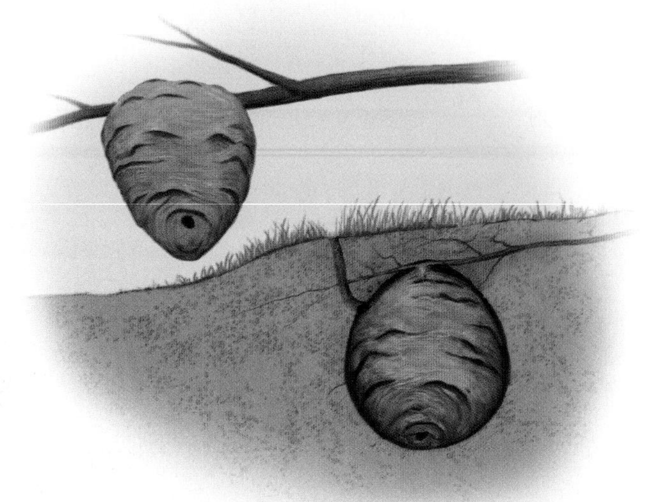

Thank you to beekeepers Rosie and Jim Lonborg,
American League Cy Young award winner, 1967.
—J.P.

Thank you to N.C. Wyeth.
—R.B.

ISBN 978-0-545-45190-1

12 11 10 15 16 17 18/0

Printed in the U.S.A. 40
First printing, September 2013

What would happen if a hornet came face-to-face with a wasp? What if they had a fight? Who do you think would win? Learn facts. Make a prediction!

MEET A HORNET

I am an Asian giant hornet. My scientific name is *Vespa mandarinia*. There are about 2,000 different types of hornets. I am one of the largest and most aggressive hornets—I sting multiple times.

ACTUAL SIZE

AMAZING

The Asian giant hornet is the largest in the world.

Don't call me a bee. I'm not a bee, and I don't make honey. I am a hornet!

I am a wasp. I am slightly orange and have a skinny waist. I am a paper wasp, and my scientific name is *Polistes perplexus*. Don't come near me, or I might sting you.

ACTUAL SIZE

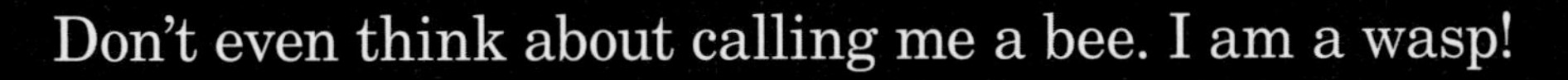

INSECTS

Ants, bees, hornets, and wasps are similar. Scientists say they are related. Their bodies have three parts:

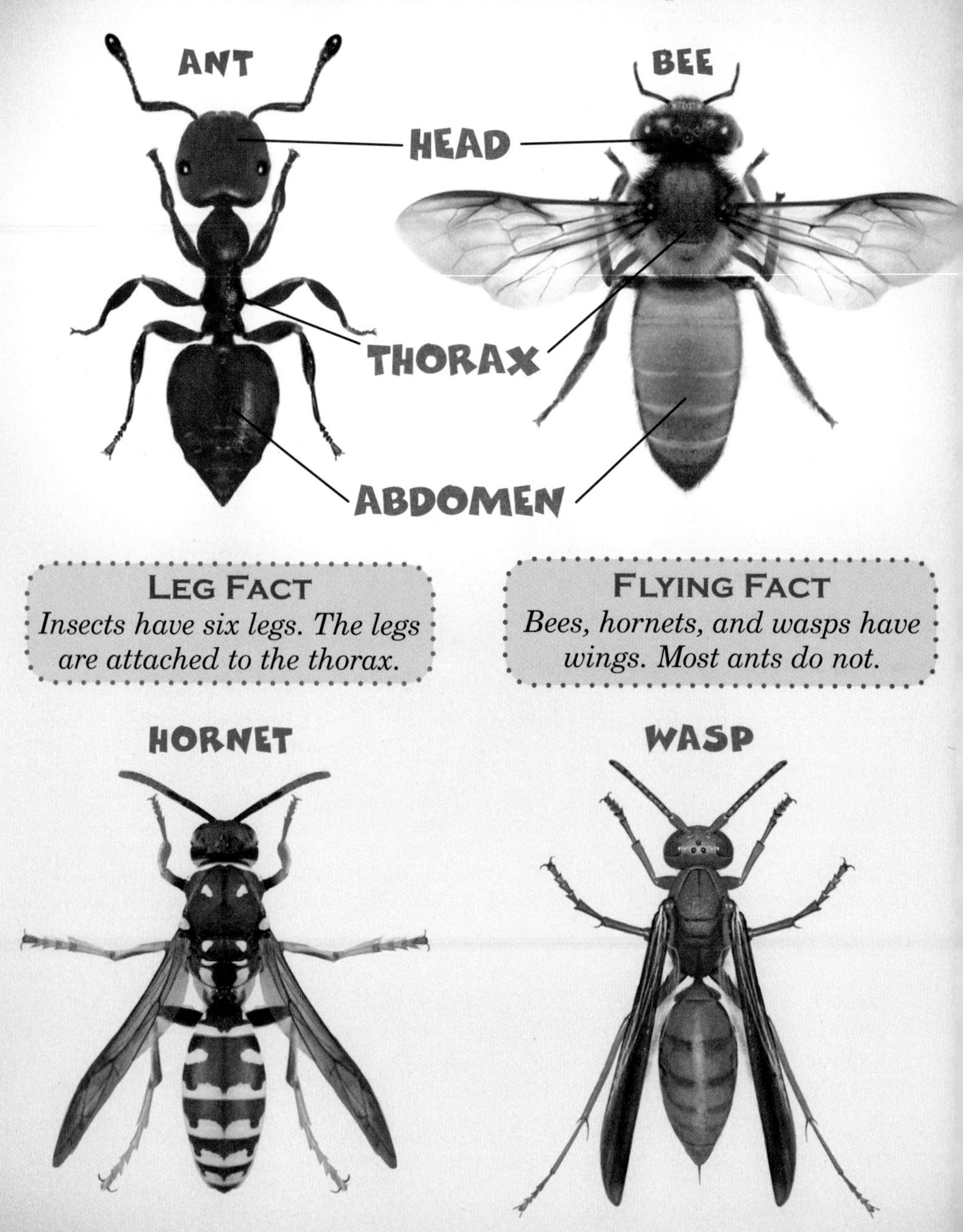

LEG FACT
Insects have six legs. The legs are attached to the thorax.

FLYING FACT
Bees, hornets, and wasps have wings. Most ants do not.

Look at their bodies. All four insects have a similar body type.

COMPARE

A spider body has two parts—cephalothorax and abdomen.

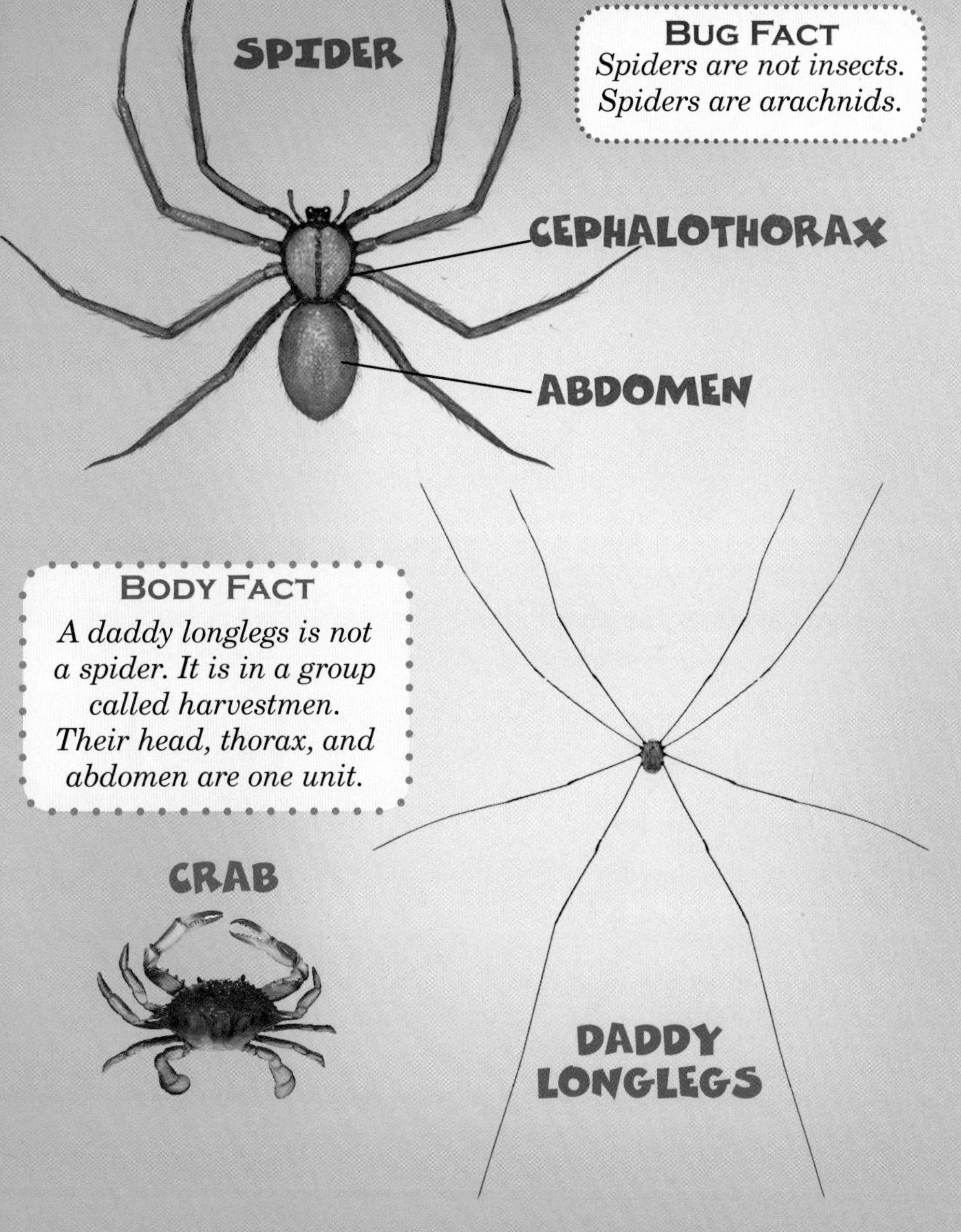

BUG FACT
Spiders are not insects. Spiders are arachnids.

BODY FACT
A daddy longlegs is not a spider. It is in a group called harvestmen. Their head, thorax, and abdomen are one unit.

A crab also has its head, thorax, and abdomen as one unit.

BEES

Bees pollinate plants. These insects pick up pollen (a special powder) on their legs and bring it to another plant, which helps the plants reproduce.

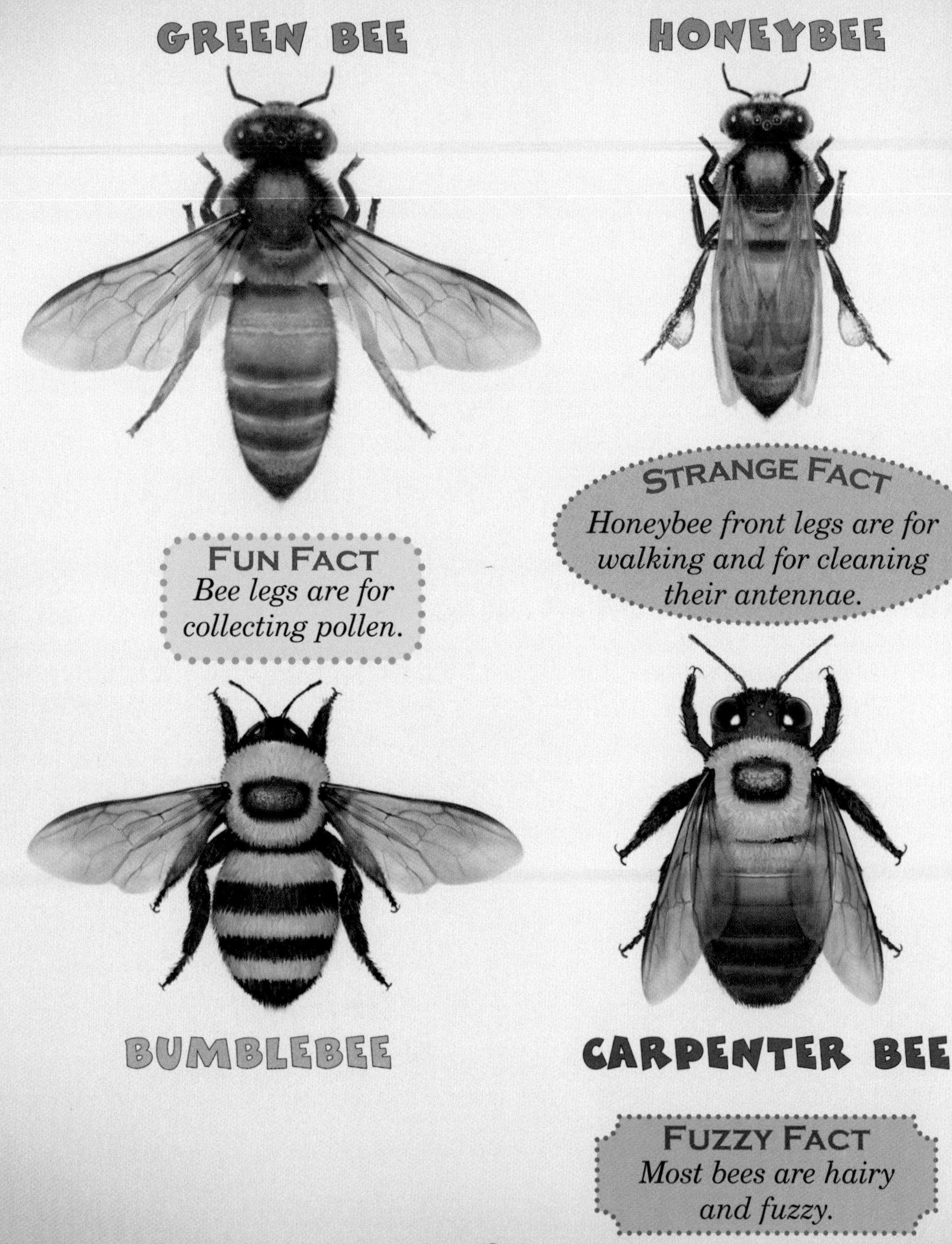

MORE ABOUT BEES

There are about 20,000 different species of bees. They live everywhere in the world where there are flowers. Bees do not live in Antarctica.

COOL FACT
Honey is bee throw-up.

COLOR FACT
Bees come in many colors.

FLOWERS

Trees, bushes, flowers, weeds, vegetables, and other plants all have flowers. The honeybee visits them all.

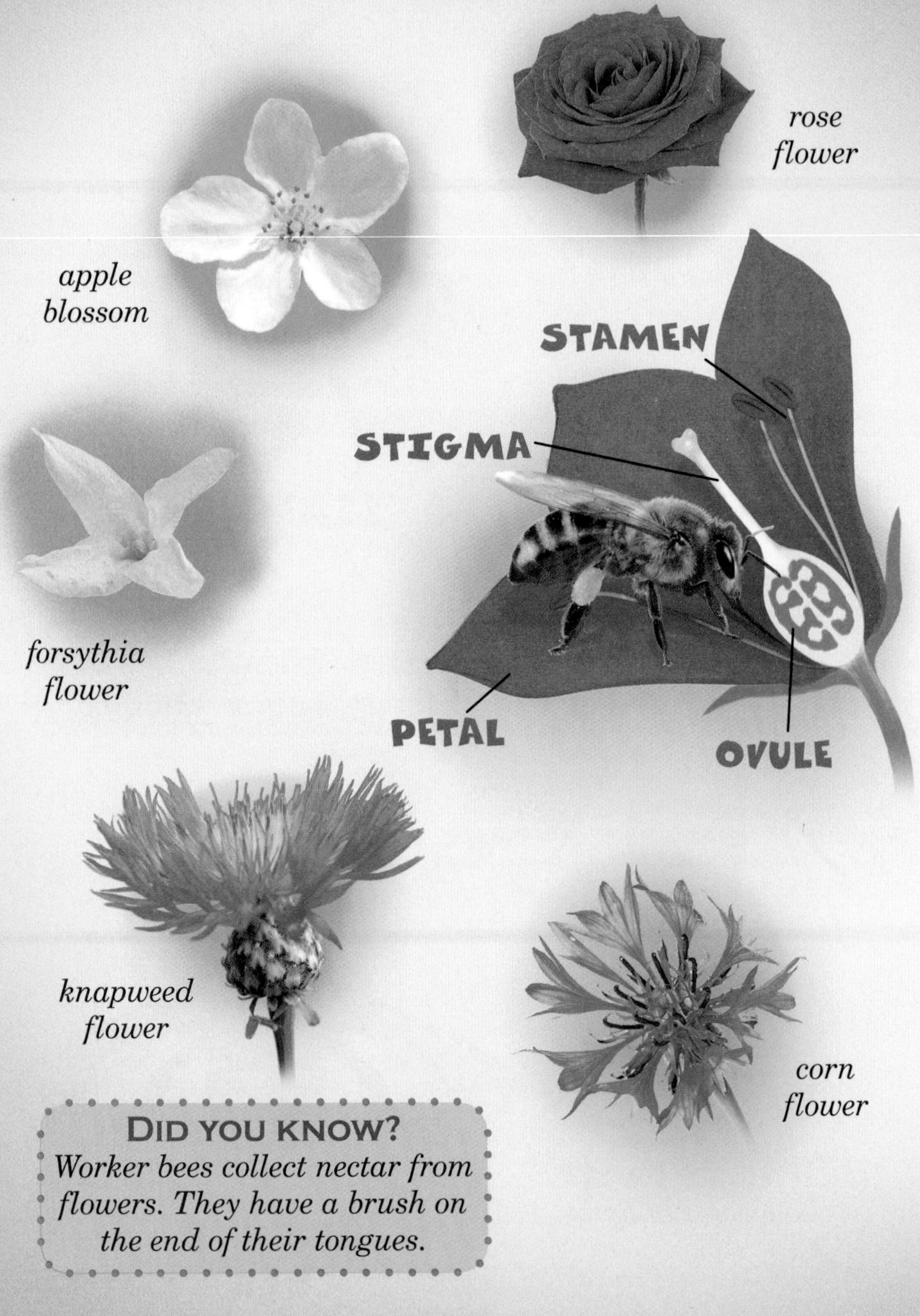

rose flower

apple blossom

forsythia flower

knapweed flower

corn flower

DID YOU KNOW?
Worker bees collect nectar from flowers. They have a brush on the end of their tongues.

Honey is sweet food that bees make for their hive. The honey is made when honeybees collect nectar from flowers and partially digest it. They then fly back to the hive and regurgitate it into the honeycomb.

DEFINITION

Regurgitate *means to throw up.*

FACT

One honeybee makes 1/12 of a teaspoon of honey in its life.

There are three types of bees in the honeybee hive: one queen bee, drones, and worker bees.

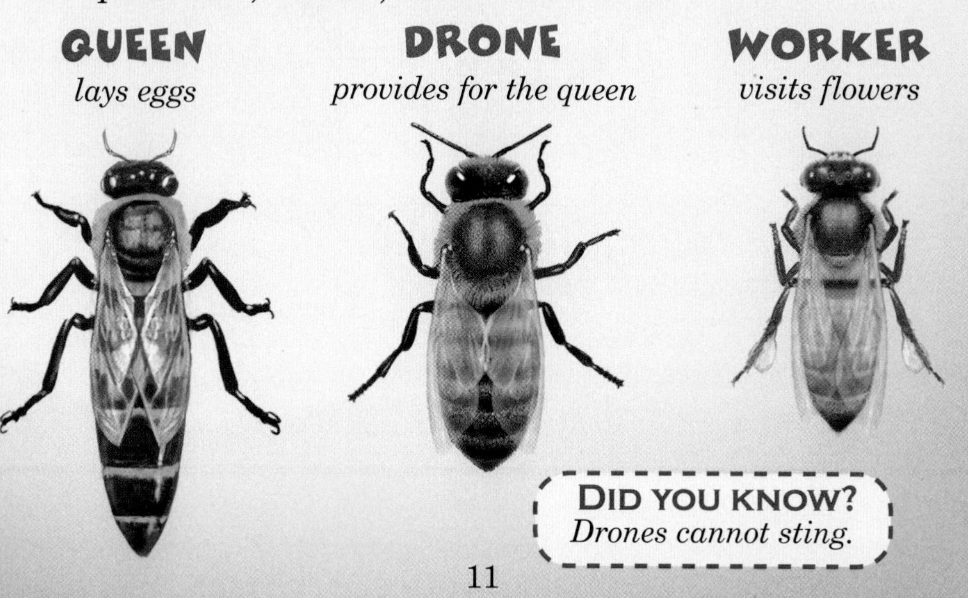

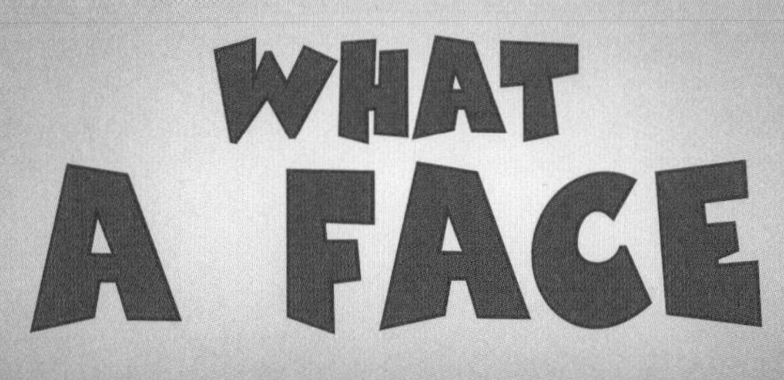

WHAT A FACE

How do you like my hornet face? I am so awesome, I should be making science-fiction movies in Hollywood. I could be a star!

DID YOU KNOW?
Hornets, wasps, and bees have compound eyes.

MOUTH FACT
Hornets have strong jaws. They bite!

AMAZING FACT
Compound eyes allow insects to see multiple images at once.

I am very aggressive. You could say that I have a bad attitude.

How do you like my wasp face? I am so good-looking, I should be a Halloween mask. I could scare you!

FACT
Wasps and hornets have compound eyes, but they also have three small eyes on the top of their heads.

BITE FACT
Wasps have strong jaws, too!

DID YOU KNOW?
Wasps and hornets can feel, taste, and hear with their antennae.

If you bother me, I also can be nasty.

HORNET HOMES

This is where I live—a hornet's nest.

PAPER NEST

SPIT FACT
Hornets chew wood with their saliva to make a paper nest.

DID YOU KNOW?
The interior of a large hornet's nest has different levels to house larvae.

UMBRELLA NEST

DEFINITION
A larva is a newly hatched insect that resembles a worm.

FUN FACT
Hornets made paper before humans.

WASP HOMES

I am a wasp, and I prefer to live underground.

UNDERGROUND NEST

FACT
Wasps dig their own tunnels or sometimes find an abandoned burrow.

UNDERGROUND PAPER NEST CROSS SECTION

Sometimes I build a mud nest. I might even build it in your house.

MUD FACT
Wasps mix dirt and spit to make mud.

DIET

Do you wonder what I eat? I am a hornet; I don't care for nectar or those goofy flowers. I like to eat other bugs.

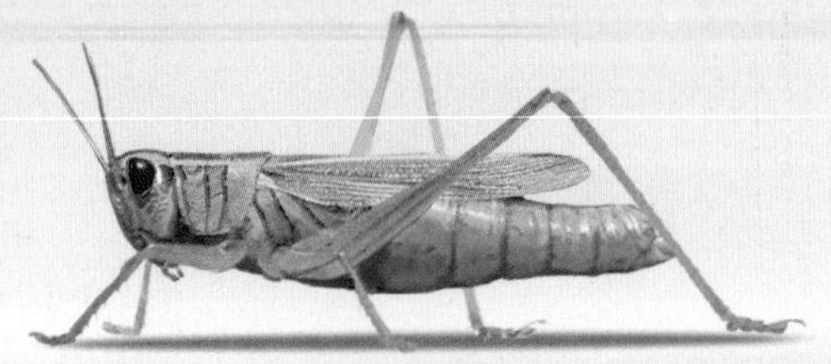

FACT
Hornets attack beehives, kill bees, and eat larvae.

I sometimes eat dead animals, or maybe your garbage.

DIET

I am a wasp. I eat meat—mostly spiders, caterpillars, bugs, and other insects. I like to eat human food, too.

FUN FACT
On a picnic, a wasp may go after your cheeseburger.

DID YOU KNOW?
A wasp would visit a flower and drink a little nectar.

TOO NASTY ! TO SHOW

Wasps like roadkill. It is common for people to find a dead snake covered with hungry wasps.

WINGS AND LEGS

Hornets have four wings. Each side of the hornet has a fore wing and a hind wing. They hook together while in flight.

DID YOU KNOW?
The wing hooks are called hamuli; they look like Velcro.

Close-up of hamuli

FUN FACT
A hornet's leg has multiple joints. Each leg has more than one knee.

THAT'S AMAZING!
A hornet can flap its wings about 10,000 times per minute.

Legs and Wings

Wasps also have four wings.

Fact
Insects do not have bones. They have an outer shell called an exoskeleton.

Wing Fact
Hornet and wasp wings are made of the same material as their exoskeleton.

Hey, buddy, I'm going to eat you soon!

HORNET STINGER

A honeybee will sting you once and then die. A hornet can sting over and over again.

FACT
The abdomen of the hornet is segmented. It can swivel around and line up a perfect sting.

This is a close-up of a hornet stinger. It has tiny ridges.

DEFINITION
Segmented *means made of different sections.*

CAN YOU?
Can you outrun a hornet? Hornets fly about 15 miles per hour.

A wasp has a smooth stinger. A wasp can also sting multiple times!

OTHER ANIMALS THAT STING
Bees, stingrays, jellyfish, platypuses, and scorpions.

This is a close-up of a wasp stinger.

SPEED FACTS
An Olympic sprinter runs 26 miles per hour. A wasp can fly up to 17 miles per hour. A third grader can run up to 12 miles per hour.

FACT
The wasp's and hornet's abdomen can swivel 360 degrees.

Just looking at the stingers can make you shiver.

HISTORY

Hornets have been on earth for more than 150 million years. Hornets and dinosaurs once lived together.

QUESTION?
How many hornets would it take to aggravate a T. rex?

Here is a hornet trapped in amber.

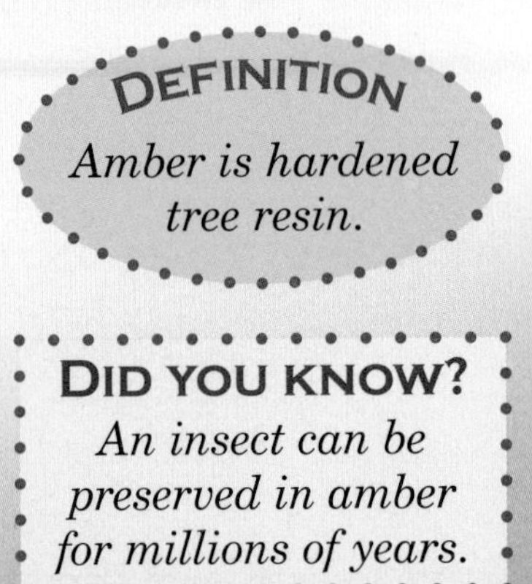

DID YOU KNOW?
An insect can be preserved in amber for millions of years.

HISTORY

FACT
Wasps also lived millions of years ago.

Would this be a good WHO WOULD WIN? book?
APATOSAURUS VS. WASP

DEFINITION
A fossil is the impression of a prehistoric plant or animal preserved in rock.

Look at this 125-million-year-old fossil. The wasp hasn't changed much. Look at the segmented body, wings, and antennae.

OTHER HORNETS

This is a fighter jet. It is called the F/A-18 Hornet. Like a hornet, it can "sting" multiple times.

AIR SHOW FACT

The Blue Angels fly F/A-18s.

F/A-18 HORNETS

The Blue Angels are the U.S. Navy's flight-demonstration team.

NAME FACT

The Sacramento State University sports teams call themselves the Hornets.

There is a U.S. Navy LHD-1 ship called the USS *Wasp*. It is an assault ship.

DID YOU KNOW?
LHD *stands for "Landing Helicopter Dock."*

FACT
Eight U.S. Navy ships have been named Wasp.

DID YOU KNOW?
There is a rugby team in England called the London Wasps.

The "wasp waist" style was fashionable in the eighteenth and nineteenth centuries.

TRUE HORNET STORY

When he was a boy, the illustrator of this book was stung by a swarm of hornets after stepping on a nest by mistake.

HORNET JEWELRY

Some people make hornet jewelry.

DEFINITION
A brooch is an ornament or jewelry that has a pin on the back.

TRUE WASP STORY

When the author of this book was in Little League, he was stung by a wasp while at bat.

The umpire thought the batter was complaining about the called third strike.

WASP JEWELRY

Would you wear a wasp ring?

DEFINITION
A necklace is jewelry worn around the neck.

ring

necklace

The hornet is flying near a dragonfly. It doesn't see the wasp flying nearby.

With no warning, the hornet attacks, but the wasp stings the hornet in the eye.

The wounded hornet flies in circles to figure out what happened. The wasp decides to fly away and avoid a battle.

The hornet darts after the wasp. It attacks and stings the wasp several times.

The wasp drops to the ground to try to escape. The hornet stings hurt! The hornet follows.

It stings the wasp two more times in the head. The wasp tries to fight back, but it can't. It is severely wounded.

The wasp dies of its wounds. The hornet's eye is injured, but the fight is over. The hornet has won.

It decides to eat the wasp.

WHO HAS THE ADVANTAGE? CHECKLIST

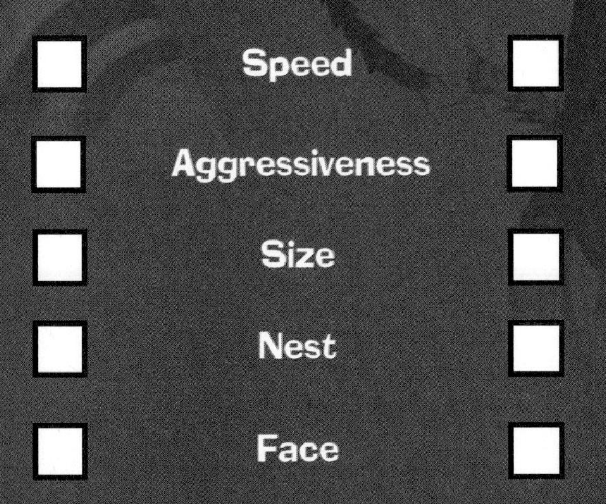

HORNET		WASP
☐	Speed	☐
☐	Aggressiveness	☐
☐	Size	☐
☐	Nest	☐
☐	Face	☐

Author note: This is one way the fight might have ended. How would you write the ending?